To:

Donna Pringle

From:

Date:

9/25/19

Happy Today

Published in Nashville, Tennessee, by Thomas Nelson. Thomas Nelson is a registered trademark of HarperCollins Christian Publishing, Inc.

Thomas Nelson titles may be purchased in bulk for educational, business, fund-raising, or sales promotional use. For information, please e-mail SpecialMarkets@ ThomasNelson.com.

Unless otherwise noted, Scripture quotations are taken from the New King James Version®. © 1982 by Thomas Nelson. Used by permission. All rights reserved.

Other Scripture references are from the following sources: Contemporary English Version (CEV), copyright © 1991, 1992, 1995 by American Bible Society. Used by permission. English Standard Version (ESV), 2001 by Crossway, a publishing ministry of Good News Publishers. Used by permission. All rights reserved. Good News Translation in Today's English Version—Second Edition (GNT). Copyright 1992 by American Bible Society. Used by permission. *The Message* (MSG). Copyright © by Eugene H. Peterson 1993, 1994, 1995, 1996, 2000, 2001, 2002. Used by permission of NavPress. All rights reserved. Represented by Tyndale House Publishers, Inc. New American Standard Bible® (NASB, 1977). Copyright © 1960, 1962, 1963, 1968, 1971, 1972, 1973, 1975, 1977 by The Lockman Foundation. Used by permission. (www.Lockman.org). New Century Version® (NCV). © 2005 by Thomas Nelson. Used by permission. All rights reserved. Holy Bible, New International Version®, NIV®. Copyright © 1973, 1978, 1984, 2011 by Biblica, Inc.® Used by permission of Zondervan. All rights reserved worldwide. www. zondervan.com. Holy Bible, New Living Translation (NLT). © 1996, 2004, 2007, 2013, 2015 by Tyndale House Foundation. Used by permission of Tyndale House Publishers, Inc., Carol Stream, Illinois 60188. All rights reserved. Revised Standard Version of the Bible (RSV), copyright 1946, 1952, and 1971 National Council of the Churches of Christ in the United States of America. Used by permission. All rights reserved. The Living Bible (TLB). Copyright © 1971. Used by permission of Tyndale House Publishers, Inc., Carol Stream, Illinois 60188. All rights reserved. The Voice™ (THE VOICE). © 2012 by Ecclesia Bible Society. Used by permission. All rights reserved. Note: Italics in quotations from The Voice are used to "indicate words not directly tied to the dynamic translation of the original language" but that "bring out the nuance of the original, assist in completing ideas, and . . . provide readers with information that would have been obvious to the original audience" (The Voice, preface).

ISBN 978-1-4002-1724-3

Printed in China

19 20 21 22 23   DSC   10 9 8 7 6 5 4 3 2 1

Happy Today

A GUIDED JOURNAL TO
Genuine Joy

MAX LUCADO

THOMAS NELSON
Since 1798

Happy Again

*J*oy seems to be in short supply. Everyone looks for it, but few seem to find it. According to one study, only 33 percent of Americans described themselves as "happy".[1] How could this be? We enjoy unprecedented medical advancements and technological luxuries, yet two-thirds of us live under a gray cloud.

Let's see what we can do about it. This book is a guided journal to help you find genuine joy. Happiness is available. Finding it may take some work and redirection of habits, but it is yours for the seeking. Make happiness your quest. Take time to pause, reflect, journal, breathe, and, in doing so, create a pathway to genuine joy.

It all begins by managing the way you see people.

Jesus was once asked to state the greatest command. If only He had done just that. If only Jesus had stopped with one command. One was sufficient. One would have been enough. No one would have complained or asked for a second command. In fact, only one was requested. A religious leader asked him:

"Of all the commandments, which is the most important?"

"The most important one," answered Jesus, "is this: 'Hear, O Israel: The Lord our God, the Lord is one. Love the Lord your God with all of your heart and with all your soul and with all your mind and with all your strength.' The second is this: 'Love your neighbor as you love yourself.' There is no commandment greater than these." (Mark 12:28–31 NIV)

How many answers did the man seek? One.
How many did he receive? Two!

If Jesus had stopped with one command, we would be satisfied. But he didn't. He offered a second, and it's a doozy. "The second is this: 'Love your neighbor as you love yourself'" (Mark 12:31 NIV).

With one sentence, Jesus brought home the pathway to genuine joy. He brought it right into the middle of traffic jams and conference meetings and greeting strangers and meeting neighbors and loving kids.

"It is more blessed to give than to receive" (Acts 20:35). Indeed, loving people is good for us.

People? Aren't people the problem standing in the way of your happiness? Try to find a parking place, and you can't. Why? People. Try to get in to see the doctor, and the next opening is two years from Thursday. Why? People.

All of life's ups and downs can be traced back to people. Car pileups. Moral letdowns. System foul-ups. Emotional breakdowns. System snarl-ups. Verbal dress downs. All because there are so many people.

No wonder the Bible has so much to say about finding joy in the act of sharing it. Happiness happens when you give it away.

God's solution for the ills of society is a quorum of unselfish, life-giving, God-loving folks who flow through neighborhoods and businesses like cleansing agents, bringing in the good and flushing out the bad.

Everyone else shows up at work with a scowl and a list of things to get done. But you? You still have your work to accomplish, but you also have this pursuit: *Whom can I help today? Which person can I encourage? Who needs a little sunshine?*

Maybe the new employee who occupies the cubicle down the hall. Or the neighbor whose Chihuahua wanders into your yard.

Or your teacher. Yes, your teacher. The one who sucks lemons for breakfast and devours students for lunch. Others avoid her. Not you. You look for ways to lift her spirits, brighten her day, compliment her, understand her, and thank her.

The world, and your world, will be different because you tried.

"Love your neighbor as yourself." Let's put the command of Christ to the test. Let's make others happy and see if we aren't the ones who are the happiest.

How to Find Happiness

*H*umans are on a hunt. While our ancestors once hunted for food and shelter, the object of our quest is different. Today many of us spend our lives frantically looking for happiness. It is the golden ticket. If only we could find it, we would be, well, happy. But where is happiness? When will we find it? When we have the perfect job, partner, or financial situation? When we arrive at a certain weight, status, or neighborhood?

While we all want to find happiness, the search is exhausting. Even when we do feel happy, it's only for a moment, and then something happens that steals our happiness. Because of this, the next time we feel happy, we also feel afraid that the happiness will go away, making even happiness itself less happy.

But what if happiness didn't have to be this way—difficult to find and easy to lose? What if we could feel happy every day?

In the book of Acts, Jesus is recorded as saying, "It is more blessed to give than to receive" (Acts 20:35). This truth turns the pursuit of happiness around. Instead of pursuing happiness for yourself, Jesus said to pursue happiness for someone else. In turn, you will experience the feelings of happiness.

Want to know how to find happiness? Happiness happens when you give it away.

And this isn't superficial happiness. This is the type of joy that won't disappear when the money, job, or house does.

If you are going to find the joy that comes through giving joy away, you need a plan—practical principles for making happiness happen. Let's embark on a happiness project.

ONE

*S*cripture has more than twenty-seven hundred passages that contain words like *joy, happiness, gladness, merriment, pleasure, celebration, cheer, laughter, delight, jubilation, feasting, blessing,* and *exultation.*[1] Our joy level matters to God.

This is no call to naiveté or superficial happy talk. Jesus spoke candidly about sin, death, and the needs of the human heart. Yet he did so with hope. His purpose statement read, "I came to give life with joy and abundance" (John 10:10 THE VOICE). Jesus was happy and wants us to be the same.

> And the angel said to them, "Be not afraid; for behold, I bring you good news of a great joy which will come to all the people; for to you is born this day in the city of David a Savior, who is Christ the Lord."
>
> —Luke 2:10–11 RSV

14

What does *happiness* mean to you? What words, feelings, or images come to mind when you think about being happy?

. . . .

. . . .

. . . .

. . . .

. . . .

. . . .

. . . .

. . . .

. . . .

. . . .   *Happiness.*

. . . .   *Everyone craves*

. . . .   *it. And everyone*

                                                                                   benefits from it.

15

*H*ow long has it been since you felt a level of contagious, infectious, unflappable, unstoppable happiness? Maybe your answer is "I feel that way all the time." If so, God bless you. For many, perhaps most of us, the answer is "Well, it's been a while. I used to be happy, but then life took its toll."

"The disease took my health."

"The economy took my job."

"The jerk took my heart."

And as a result something pilfered our happiness. It can seem such a fragile thing, this joy. Still we keep searching for it, longing for it. That's what this book is meant to help you find: the unexpected door to joy.

Sing praise to the LORD, you saints of His,
And give thanks at the remembrance of His holy name.
For His anger is but for a moment,
His favor is for life;
Weeping may endure for a night,
But joy comes in the morning.

—Psalm 30:4–5

Write about the last time you felt truly happy. What were the circumstances in your life? If the happiness has since faded, why do you think that is?

....

....

....

....   *How do we*

....   *explain the*

....   *gloom? We*

....   *are using the*

....   *wrong door.*

....

....

....

....

....

THREE

The oft-used front door to happiness is the one described by the advertising companies: acquire, retire, and aspire to drive faster, dress trendier, and drink more.

Yet for all its promise, it fails to deliver. There is another option. But you might need to change doors.

The motto on the front door says "Happiness happens when you get." The sign on the lesser-used back door counters "Happiness happens when you give."

"It is more blessed to give than to receive."

—Acts 20:35

Write about a time you did something kind for someone else.
What motivated you to do this? How did it make you feel?

....

....

....

....

....

....

....

....

....

....   *Seeking joy?*

....   *Do good for*

....   *someone else.*

FOUR

esus was accused of much, but he was never, ever described as a grump, sourpuss, or self-centered jerk. People didn't groan when he appeared.

He called them by name.

He listened to their stories.

He answered their questions.

He visited their sick relatives and helped their sick friends.

Thousands came to hear him. Hundreds chose to follow him. They shut down their businesses and walked away from careers to be with him. He brought joy to the people of first-century Palestine. And he wants to bring joy to the people of this generation, and he has enlisted some special agents of happiness to do the job—you and me.

"The thief approaches with malicious intent, looking to steal, slaughter, and destroy; I came to give life with joy and abundance. I am the good shepherd."

—John 10:10–11 THE VOICE

Does the idea of Jesus being happy, attending parties, smiling, and laughing make you uncomfortable? Why or why not?

....

....

....

....

....

....

....

....

Happiness happens when you give it away.

....

....

....

....

....

ou can't control your genetics. You aren't in charge of the weather, the traffic, or the occupant of the White House. But you can always increase the number of smiles on our planet. You can lower the anger level in your city. You—yes, you—can help people to sleep better, laugh more, hum instead of grumble, walk instead of stumble. You can lighten the load and brighten the day of other human beings. And don't be surprised when you begin to sense a newfound joy yourself.

"A new commandment I give to you, that you love one another; as I have loved you, that you also love one another. By this all will know that you are My disciples."

—John 13:34–35

What areas of your life feel like they're out of your control?
Do you believe you're able to affect your own happiness as
well as the happiness of those around you?

....

....

....

....

....

....

....

....

....

....

Doing good

....

does good

....

for the doer.

SIX

You and I indwell a lonely planet. Broken hearts populate every office building. Discouragement mummifies countless lives. The world is desperate—yes, desperate—for a cavalry of kindness. We cannot solve every problem in society, but we can bring smiles to a few faces. And who knows? If you brighten your corner of the world and I do the same in mine, a quiet revolution of joy might break out.

"You are the light of the world. A city that is set on a hill cannot be hidden."

—Matthew 5:14

In what ways could you brighten your corner of the world this week? List three things you can do now.

....

....

....

....

....

....

....

....

....

....

....

....

Desire a rain shower of joy? Weary of the drudgery of the day to day? Then do this: make someone happy.

Find Happiness by Encouraging One Another

Even the most confident and self-assured among us needs to feel encouraged from time to time. When you're having a bad day at work, a kind word from a coworker can turn things around. When you're frustrated with your kids, encouragement from a loved one can give you what you need to get through the rest of the day. A note or a text from a friend. A neighbor complimenting your lawn. Encouragement is a simple but powerful way to make someone happy.

The Bible often talks about encouragement, *encouraging* us to encourage one another. But in scripture, encouragement is more than a high five or "Way to go!"

First Thessalonians 5:11 says, "Therefore encourage one another and build each other up" (NIV). The Greek word translated as encouragement is *paraklēsis*. *Paraklēsis* is a combination of two words: *para*, which means by the side, and *kaleō*, which means to call.[1] This definition tells us that biblical encouragement is twofold. It's coming alongside someone and calling out their potential. You don't just encourage someone for who they are but for who they could be.

When the body of Christ truly encourages one another, in a *paraklēsis* kind of way, we build each up and propel each other forward.

Over the next few weeks you'll have an opportunity to reflect on how you've been encouraged by others and how you could encourage other people, in turn feeling encouraged yourself.

SEVEN

When Jesus introduced the Holy Spirit to us in John 14–16, he called him the *parakletos*, the noun form of the very word for encouragement.[1]

Scripture encourages us. "The Scriptures were written to teach and encourage us by giving us hope" (Romans 15:4 CEV).

The saints in heaven encourage us. "Therefore, since we are surrounded by such a huge crowd of witnesses . . . let us run with endurance the race God has set before us" (Hebrews 12:1 NLT). A multitude of God's children is urging us on. Like spectators in the stands, a "crowd of witnesses" applauds from the heavens, calling on us to finish strong.

May the God who gives endurance and encouragement give you the same attitude of mind toward each other that Christ Jesus had.

—Romans 15:5 NIV

Write about how you have felt encouraged by scripture or people in your life.

....

....

....

....

....

....

....

....

....

....

....

....

God places a premium on encouragement.

EIGHT

esus asked his followers, "Who do you say that I am?"
Peter spoke up: "You are the Christ, the Son of the living God" (Matthew 16:16).

Jesus all but jumped for joy at the confession. "Blessed are you, Simon Bar-Jonah" (Matthew 16:17).

He even changed the apostle's name. Simon would now be called Peter, a name that is next of kin to *petros* or Rocky. Simon, the man who expressed rock-solid faith, needed a rock-solid name.

Jesus did to Peter what encouragers do. He summoned the best. He built Peter up.

"Blessed are you, Simon Bar-Jonah, for flesh and blood has not revealed this to you, but My Father who is in heaven. And I also say to you that you are Peter, and on this rock I will build My church, and the gates of Hades shall not prevail against it."

—Matthew 16:17–18

Consider how Jesus encouraged Peter. Write down words of encouragement you need to hear from Jesus today.

....

....

....

....   With the skill of

....   stone masons,

....   encouragers stack

....   stones of affirmation

....   and inspiration.

....

....

....

....   HELLO
                                                     _____
....   _____
                                                     _____

....

*T*hree years into my role as senior minister of our church, a former senior minister returned, not only to live in our city but also to serve on our staff. Charles Prince was thirty years my senior, Harvard educated, and a member of the Mensa society. I was in my midthirties, a rookie. The relationship could have been awkward and intimidating, but Charles preempted any stress with a visit to my office, during which he said, "I'm going to be your biggest cheerleader."

Such encouragement has a Michelangelo impact on people. The sculptor saw the figure of David within the marble and carved it out.

Let us consider how we may spur one another on toward love and good deeds, not giving up meeting together, as some are in the habit of doing, but encouraging one another.

—Hebrews 10:24–25 NIV

Write about a time someone older or wiser than you had a
Michelangelo impact on your life. What did that person say
or do to encourage you?

....

....

....

....

....

....

....

....

....

....   The encourager

....   sees your best self

....   and calls it out.

TEN

A little boy said these words to his father: "Dad, let's play darts. I'll throw, and you say 'Wonderful!'"

Every person needs to hear a "wonderful." Here is why. A *dis*couragement conspiracy is afoot. Companies spend billions of dollars to convince us that we are deficient and inadequate. To sell face cream, they tell us that our faces are wrinkled. To sell new clothes, they pronounce that our clothes are out of fashion. Marketing companies deploy the brightest minds and deepest pockets of our generation to convince us that we are chubby, smelly, ugly, and out-of-date. We are under attack!

Take up the whole armor of God, that you may be able to withstand in the evil day, and having done all, to stand. Stand therefore, having girded your waist with truth.

—Ephesians 6:13–14

Create two columns. Label the left column *Lies* and the right column *Truth*. In the left column write lies you have believed about yourself that discourage you. In the right column write a truth from God that would combat that lie with encouragement.

....

....

....

....

....

....

....

....

.... *Inadequacy*

.... *indwells a*

.... *billion hearts.*

ELEVEN

Look the Simon Peters of your world in the eye, and call forth the Rocky within them by . . .

Listening intently. A desperate woman once came to see Jesus. She was out of doctors, money, and hope. Threading her arm through the crowd, she reached the hem of his garment. And when she touched the hem of him, the bleeding stopped. "'Who touched me?' Jesus asked" (Luke 8:45 NIV). "She came shaking with fear and knelt down in front of Jesus. Then she told him the whole story" (Mark 5:33 CEV).

Do this for someone. Ask someone to tell you his—or her—story.

She came shaking with fear and knelt down in front of Jesus. Then she told him the whole story. Jesus said to the woman, "You are now well because of your faith. May God give you peace!"

—Mark 5:33–34 CEV

Write about a time someone encouraged you by listening to your whole story.

. . . .

. . . .

. . . .

. . . .

. . . .

. . . .

. . . .

Give someone the rarest of gifts: your full attention.

. . . .

. . . .

. . . .

. . . .

. . . .

. . . .

*L*ook the Simon Peters of your world in the eye, and call forth the Rocky within them by . . .

Praising abundantly. Biblical encouragement is no casual, kind word but rather a premeditated resolve to lift the spirit of another person. "Let us consider how we may spur one another on toward love and good deeds" (Hebrews 10:24 NIV). The verb *consider* means "to perceive clearly . . . understand fully, consider closely."[1]

Do you know someone who needs unbridled encouragement? Of course you do. Here is an idea. Call a friend or relative, and begin the conversation with these words: "Can I have 120 seconds to tell you what a great person you are?" Then let it loose. Build him up. Affirm her. Embarrass him with praise. Drench her with words of encouragement.

Look for the best in each other, and always do your best to bring it out.

—1 Thessalonians 5:15 THE MESSAGE

Think of a friend or family member who needs encouragement. Write a few sentences praising his or her character.

....

....

....

....

....

Everyone needs

....

a cheerleader.

....

So be one.

....

....

....

....

....

....

Find Happiness by Accepting One Another

People are annoying, aren't they? They say the wrong thing at the wrong time. They have the wrong opinion, the wrong political affiliation. They're a part of the wrong church denomination.

If only everybody could be like us, think like us, act like us, then life would be easy and happy.

Unfortunately, this is never going to happen. God did not create two people the same. We are diverse in culture, skin color, beliefs, and behaviors, and we were meant to be this way. Because of this, if you think anyone who behaves or thinks differently than you do is a nuisance, life will be pretty miserable.

Jesus often hung out with those who were considered different. His disciples were not the popular jocks. They were fishermen and ex-tax collectors. He spent time with children. He talked with women in public—something Jewish men didn't do in first-century Palestine. Jesus did not attempt to build a tribe of others just like him. He broke through tribal barriers. Jesus accepted and embraced others.

We have a choice to do the same. We can either feel annoyed and angry with others, or we can accept them for being beautifully different from us. We can either feel irritated, or we can do as scripture says and "Be patient, bearing with one another in love" (Ephesians 4:2 NIV).

Happiness doesn't happen when everyone becomes just like you. Happiness happens when we accept one another and, instead of rejecting our differences, embrace them.

THIRTEEN

*W*hat pets your peeve?

The phrases we use regarding our pet peeves reveal the person who actually suffers. He "gets under my skin" or "gets on my nerves," or she is such a "pain in my neck." Whose skin, nerves, and neck? Ours! Who suffers? We do! Every pet peeve writes a check on our joy account.

Suppose a basket of Ping-Pong balls represents your daily quota of happiness. Each aggravation, if you allow it, can snatch a ball out of your basket. How can you help people smile if you have a hole in your happiness basket? You can't.

Therefore, as God's chosen people, holy and dearly loved, clothe yourselves with compassion, kindness, humility, gentleness and patience. Bear with each other and forgive one another if any of you has a grievance against someone. Forgive as the Lord forgave you.

—Colossians 3:12–13 NIV

Write about a time someone got on your nerves. What did
this person do to annoy you, and how did it make you feel
physically, mentally, and emotionally?

Arson (Allen)

Joy is such a
precious commodity.
Why squander it
on a quibble?

FOURTEEN

The apostle Paul said, "Be patient, bearing with one another in love" (Ephesians 4:2 NIV).

The apostle's word for *patient* is a term that combines "long" and "tempered."[1] The short-tempered person has a hair-trigger reaction. The patient person is "long tempered." The word *tempered* literally means "taking a long time to boil."[2] In other words, not quickly overheated.

The patient person sees all the peculiarities of the world. But rather than react, he bears with them.

Be patient, bearing with one another in love.

—Ephesians 4:2 NIV

Write about what type of person you are—patient or impatient. Do you like this about yourself? Why or why not?

....

....

....

....

....

....

....

....

....

....

....

....

Irks come with life, but they need not diminish life.

FIFTEEN

My wife, Denalyn, is the happiest person within a dozen zip codes. Ask her friends or ask my daughters. They will tell you she's married to an odd duck, but she has the joy level of a kid at a carnival. Here is her secret: She's learned to enjoy my idiosyncrasies. She thinks I'm entertaining. Who would've thought?

To be clear, she lets her opinions be heard. I know when I've tested her patience. Yet I never fear failing the test and am happier for it.

Happiness is less an emotion and more a decision—a decision to bear with one another.

Love is patient, love is kind . . . it is not easily angered, it keeps no record of wrongs.

—1 Corinthians 13:4–5 NIV

Write about someone you love—a family member, friend, spouse, or partner. Write about this person's annoying or odd behaviors as well as the reasons you love him or her.

....

....

....

....

....

....

....

....

....

....

....

....

....

Happiness is less an emotion and more a decision.

SIXTEEN

Don't people bear with you? The next time you find it difficult to live with others, imagine what it is like to live with you.

Or, to use the lingo of Jesus, don't obsess about the speck of dust in another person's eye while ignoring the plank in your own eye (Matthew 7:3–5).

We have eagle-eye vision when it comes to others but can be blind as moles when we examine ourselves. Were we to be honest, brutally honest, don't we spend more time trying to fix others than we should? Don't we have more expertise on the faults of our friends than the faults of ourselves?

"Why do you notice the little piece of dust in your friend's eye, but you don't notice the big piece of wood in your own eye? . . . First, take the wood out of your own eye. Then you will see clearly to take the dust out of your friend's eye."

—Matthew 7:3,5 NCV

List some idiosyncrasies or annoying behaviors that someone close to you might point out. Write about how it feels to be accepted by this person despite your flaws.

· ·

· ·

· ·

· ·

·   *If you want*

·   *to change the*

·   *world, begin*

                                                                            with yourself.

· ·

· ·

· ·

· ·

· ·

· ·

SEVENTEEN

The clear majority of details in the world are simply that—details. Small stuff. Don't sweat the small stuff, and you won't sweat much at all.

During the next few days, you'll be tested. A driver will forget to turn on his blinker. A shopper will have fifteen items in the "ten items or less" checkout line. Your husband is going to blow his nose like a foghorn. Your wife is going to take her half of the garage in the middle. When they do, think about your Ping-Pong ball basket.

Don't give up a single ball.

For You formed my inward parts;
You covered me in my mother's womb.
I will praise You, for I am fearfully *and* wonderfully made.

—Psalm 139:13–14

Over the course of twenty-four hours, each time you get annoyed by someone, think about that person as a unique child of God, fearfully and wonderfully made. Record how this affected your day.

··

··

··

··

··

··

··

··

·····························   *No pet peeve is*

·····························   *worth your joy or*

·····························   *another person's.*

Find Happiness in Humility

ocial media has trained us to expect a positive response to everything we do. Got a new haircut? *Like.* Took the dog on a walk? *Like.* Went on vacation? *Like.* Because of this, we often fall into a performance way of living, one that puts a premium on *likes* and applause over humility and work behind the scenes.

Martha fell into this performance way of living. When Jesus went to visit her and her sister, Mary, Martha did the behind the scenes work in the kitchen, preparing the meal, while Mary sat at Jesus' feet. Martha wasn't happy about this. But when she complained to Jesus, he had an interesting response. He did not applaud Martha or tell her how delicious her food was. Instead, he told her to take the focus off herself: "There is only one thing worth being concerned about" (Luke 10:42 NLT).

That *one thing* is not recognition or Facebook likes. That *one thing* is whom Mary was sitting by—Jesus.

If your happiness depends on recognition or social media attention, happiness will come and go. If serving others is only worth it if you get appreciation in return, you will not be a happy servant. But if you can shift your mind-set away from the performance-centered life and toward a Christ-centered one, performance will give way to humility. You won't need attention from everybody else because you will be satisfied with the attention Christ gives you as you sit at his feet.

Christ did not call us to live big, loud, popular lives. He called us to follow him. Whether that's onto a stage or into obscurity, faithful Christ followers are humble enough to let Jesus, not ego, lead the way.

EIGHTEEN

*W*hat had happened to hospitable Martha, welcoming Martha? Luke gives us the answer. "Martha was distracted by the big dinner she was preparing" (Luke 10:40 NLT). She had *big* plans to make a *big* impression with her *big* event. Instead she made a *big* mess. She became "worried and upset over all these details!" (v. 41 NLT).

What is the lesson behind Martha's meltdown? That it's a sin to cook? That hospitality is the Devil's tool? No.

Martha's downfall was not her work or request; it was her motivation. I can't help but think that she wasn't serving Jesus; she was performing for him. She wasn't making a meal for him; she was making a big deal about her service. She was suckered in with the subtlest of lies: self-promotion.

The Lord said to her, "My dear Martha, you are worried and upset over all these details! There is only one thing worth being concerned about. Mary has discovered it, and it will not be taken away from her."

—Luke 10:41–42 NLT

Write about how you identify with Martha. Do you ever crave recognition? How do you feel when you don't get the recognition you think you deserve?

....

....

....

.... *Martha was in*

.... *the presence of the*

.... *Prince of Peace,*

.... *yet she was the*

.... *picture of stress.*

....

....

....

....

....

NINETEEN

*I*t's a slippery slope, this thing of self-promotion. What begins as a desire to serve Christ metastasizes into an act of impressing people. When that happens, gifted Marthas become miserable mumblers. It's easy to see why. If your happiness depends on the applause and approval of others, you'll yo-yo up and down, based on the fickle opinion of people. If noticed, you'll strut. If unnoticed, you'll grumble.

Do nothing out of selfish ambition.

—Philippians 2:3 NIV

Even the good deeds we do in the name of Christ can secretly
be for ourselves. Have you done an act of service that was
actually motivated by selfish ambition? Write about that
experience and how it affected your happiness.

....

....

....

....

....

....

....

....

....   *Self-promotion*

....   *is all about*

....   *self.*

TWENTY

When ministry becomes vain ambition, nothing good happens.

I am not God's MVP.

You are not God's MVP.

We are not God's gift to humanity. He loves us and indwells us and has great plans for us. We are valuable but not indispensable.

Can the ax boast greater power than the person who uses it?
Is the saw greater than the person who saws?
Can a rod strike unless a hand moves it?
Can a wooden cane walk by itself? (Isaiah 10:15 NLT)

We are the ax, the saw, the rod, and the cane. We do nothing apart from the hand of God.

"Is the saw greater than the person who saws?"

—Isaiah 10:15 NLT

Write down your thoughts on Isaiah 10:15 and the idea that we do nothing apart from the hand of God. How does this make you feel? Do you have a positive or negative reaction to this passage, and why?

....
....
....
God can use
....
each of us, but
....
he doesn't need
....
any of us.
....
....
....
....
....
....

TWENTY-ONE

*H*ow wise of us to remember Paul's antidote for joy-sucking self-promotion: "With humility of mind let each of you regard one another as more important than himself" (Philippians 2:3 NASB, 1977).

Jesus surely had a smile on his face when he gave the following instructions: "When you're invited to dinner, go and sit at the last place. Then when the host comes he may very well say, 'Friend, come up to the front.' That will give the dinner guests something to talk about!" (Luke 14:10 THE MESSAGE).

Expecting the applause of others is a fool's enterprise! Do yourself a favor and assume nothing. If you go unnoticed, you won't be surprised. If you are noticed, you can celebrate.

With humility of mind let each of you regard one another as more important than himself.

—Philippians 2:3 NASB, 1977

Whom do you consider more important than you? Whom do you consider less important than you? Reflect on why this is.

....

....

....

....

Happy

....

are the

....

unentitled!

....

....

....

....

....

....

....

ake a big deal out of yourself, and brace yourself for a day of disappointments. Make a big deal out of others, and expect a blue-ribbon day. You will move from joy to joy as you regard other people's success as more important than your own.

Blessed is the Christian whose focus is on others.

Miserable is the Christian whose focus is on self.

If your desire to be noticed is making you miserable, you can bet it is doing the same for others. Stop being a Martha. Get back to basics.

Rejoice with those who rejoice.

—Romans 12:15 NIV

Try this happiness experiment today: rejoice with those who rejoice. Whenever a good thing happens to someone else, instead of wishing something good had happened to you, simply be happy for that person. Record how this affected your happiness level.

....

....

....

....

....

....

....

....   *During the next twenty-*

....   *four hours, make it*

....   *your aim to celebrate*

....   *everything good that*

....   *happens to someone else.*

Find Happiness by Greeting One Another

*T*hey may be the most overlooked passages in the New Testament, seemingly offhand comments made by Paul and others as they wrote final remarks in their letters. But these passages are too prolific to be insignificant.

"Greet one another with a holy kiss" (Romans 16:16).

"Give each other a holy kiss when you meet" (1 Corinthians 16:20 NCV).

"Greet each other with a holy kiss" (2 Corinthians 13:12 NCV).

"Give each other a holy kiss when you meet" (1 Thessalonians 5:26 NCV).

"Greet one another with a kiss of love" (1 Peter 5:14).

A kiss was the customary greeting during the time and culture these letters were written, and Paul was insistent the early church make a habit of it. Perhaps Paul knew how easy it is to disregard one another and how important a simple greeting can be.

When you're having a bad day, does it make you more or less happy when the grocery store clerk takes the time to say hello? When you're visiting a new church and someone greets you at the door, do you feel more or less welcome in the sanctuary?

Greeting one another is a simple gesture, but when you are greeted by someone else, you feel seen, noticed, and cared for. When we take the time to greet others, we make them feel the same way. Greeting one another makes the greeter and the greeted equally happy.

As you reflect on this seemingly simple instruction to greet one another, you may be surprised to find just how powerful a "hello," hug, or handshake can be.

$\mathcal{P}$erhaps we need an ultimatum on society. Oh, the "rages" that rage through people: road rage, airline passenger rage, cell phone rage, checkout rage, sideline rage, parking lot rage, and even rage from drivers who honk at people on crutches.

Rudeness has reached the point where we can all relate to the sign I saw in a medical lab: "If you are grouchy, rude, impatient, or inconsiderate, there will be a $10 charge just for putting up with you."

Yes, a tariff on tackiness has its appeal. A more practical response might be the one suggested by the apostle Paul: "Greet one another with a holy kiss" (Romans 16:16).

Greet one another with a holy kiss.

—Romans 16:16

Do you typically greet someone with a handshake, hug, or high five? How does it feel to be greeted by others in this way?

. . . .

. . . .

. . . .

. . . .

. . . .

. . . .

. . . .

. . . .

. . . .

. . . .

. . . .   *What is small*
                                                                         to you may
. . . .   *be huge to*
                                                                       someone else.
. . . .

TWENTY-FOUR

Why should we be careful to greet one another?

Out of respect. Respect is a mindfulness of another person's situation. Respect notices the new kid in class and says, "Hello." Respect pauses at the desk of the receptionist and says, "Good morning." Respect refuses to hurry through the checkout line without a genuine "Good afternoon" for the cashier. Respect removes her headphones and greets the fellow passenger. Respect removes his hat to salute the competitor, and respect attempts to remove any awkwardness by welcoming the newcomer to church.

Simply greeting one another is not that hard. But it makes a significant difference.

Show proper respect to everyone, love the family of believers, fear God, honor the emperor.

—1 Peter 2:17 NIV

First Peter 2:17 instructs us to respect everyone, love fellow Christians, fear God, and honor authority. Which of these instructions is most difficult for you, and why?

....

....

....

....

....

....

....

A greeting in its purest sense is a gesture of goodwill.

....

....

....

....

....

....

TWENTY-FIVE

*T*he first beneficiary of a greeting is the one who gives it. That was the conclusion of researchers at Pennsylvania State University. Students were divided into two groups: readers and huggers. The huggers were instructed to give or receive a minimum of five hugs per day over the course of four weeks. The readers were told to record the number of hours each day they spent reading in the same month. Unsurprisingly the huggers fared better on the happiness scale than the readers. Hugging boosted the joy level of the participants.[1]

I hope to visit you and talk with you face to face, so that our joy may be complete.

—2 John 1:12 NIV

How do you feel after visiting with a friend in person rather than over the phone, text, or email? Which interaction makes you happier, and why?

....

....

....

....

....

....

....

....

....

....

.... *Huggers are*

.... *happier.*

TWENTY-SIX

*D*on't dismiss the value of a sincere salutation. Our Master was seldom more practical than when he said, "When you knock on a door, be courteous in your greeting" (Matthew 10:12 MSG). Give people a firm handshake. Make eye contact. Be sincere.

At any gathering you will find two types of people: those who arrive with the attitude that says, "I am so glad to see you" and those whose attitude says, "I am so glad you see me." It's not hard to differentiate between the two.

"Truly I tell you, whatever you did for one of the least of these brothers and sisters of mine, you did for me."

—Matthew 25:40 NIV

How would you greet Jesus if he walked into the room right now? Do you greet others in the same way? Why or why not?

. . . .

. . . .

. . . .

. . . .

. . . .

. . . .

. . . .

. . . .

Let people know you really care, and then expect the boomerang effect.

. . . .

. . . .

. . . .

. . . .

TWENTY-SEVEN

We never know when a gesture of kindness will touch a heart. Perhaps that's why Paul urged us to greet *everyone*. He did not say, "Greet the people you like" or "Greet the people you know" or "Greet the people you want to know." He said simply, "Greet one another" (Romans 16:16).

Paul modeled his appeal for unprejudiced kindness. In the thirteen verses prior, he did with his pen what he would have loved to do with his hand. He mentally went from person to person and greeted each one with a holy greeting (Romans 16:3–16). He saluted twenty-six people by name and, in some cases, their families.

"You shall love your neighbor as yourself."

—Leviticus 19:18

Similar to what Paul did in Romans 16:3–16, make a point to greet two or three people today whom you would normally not notice. Record how each person reacted and how this affected your happiness.

....

....

....

....

....

....

....

....

....

Jesus loves

....

people who

....

love his kids.

TWENTY-EIGHT

The greatest greeting in history has yet to be given. And you can be certain that salutation won't be heard over a phone or through an email. The greatest of greetings will be issued by Jesus to you in person. "You did well. You are a good and loyal servant. Because you were loyal with small things, I will let you care for much greater things. Come and share my joy with me" (Matthew 25:23 NCV).

"Well done, good and faithful servant!"

—Matthew 25:23 NIV

What would you like Jesus to say to you when he welcomes you into God's kingdom?

. . . .

. . . .

. . . .

. . . .

. . . .

. . . .

. . . .

. . . .

. . . .

. . . .

. . . .   *Experience the joy*

. . . .   *of showing people*

                                                               they matter.

Find Happiness in Prayer

When life is going well, it's easy to feel happy. You're healthy, your job is secure, your kids are happy. But when life takes a turn—illness, death, bankruptcy—happiness is replaced by fear and despair. In these moments it's easy to feel helpless and powerless over our circumstances. It's easy to forget that we have access to the God of the universe himself with this one simple but powerful tool: prayer.

When was the last time you prayed? Perhaps it was this morning or last night. Maybe it's been longer. A month, a year, you can't remember. Sometimes life feels too overwhelming to pray. How could our petty words make a difference in the grand scheme of things?

Abraham probably thought this, but he tried anyway.

In Genesis 18, Abraham begged God to spare the sin-ridden twin cities of Sodom and Gomorrah. Abraham had family there, and in a bold move, he "stood still before the LORD" (Genesis 18:22). He asked God to spare Sodom and Gomorrah if he could find enough righteous men who lived there. How did God respond? Did he scoff or laugh? No, God listened. He allowed a lowly human to intervene with his divine plan.

When we talk to God, he listens. We may not be in control, but we are not powerless. For this reason, even when our lives take a turn for the worse, we can find joy in knowing that God is watching us and listening to us. He is at work in our lives, and with the power of prayer, we can work with him.

TWENTY-NINE

*A*braham's story gives us reason to hope. He was bold with God. He did what Scripture urges us all to do: "Pray for one another, that you may be healed" (James 5:16).

Someone you know is under attack. Your neighbor is depressed. Your sibling is off track. Your child is facing an uphill challenge. You may not know what to say. You may not have resources to help. But you have this: you have prayer.

The earnest prayer of a righteous person has great power and produces wonderful results.

—James 5:16 NLT

When you pray, do you believe God is listening to you? Why or why not?

....

....

....

....

....

....

....

....

....

....

....

....   *Your prayers prompt
                                                  the response of
                                                  God in the lives of
....   those you love.*

THIRTY

When we pray for one another, we enter God's workshop, pick up a hammer, and help him accomplish his purposes.

My dad invited my brother and me to do something similar. He loved to build. He'd already constructed two homes, including the one in which we lived. But he had bigger dreams.

"You boys want to help me?" he asked. Of course we wanted to help! And so it was that my brother and I pedaled our bikes to the construction project on Alamosa Street every day after school. I could hardly handle the excitement. I was a partner with my papa.

Our heavenly Father has invited us to be his partner too.

It is God who works in you both to will and to do for His good pleasure.

—Philippians 2:13

What's an area of your life where you need to partner with God through prayer? Spend some time writing that prayer. Be specific. What do you need from God in this situation?

....

....

....

....

....

....

....

....

....

....

....

....

....

Our prayers unlock the storehouses of heaven.

THIRTY-ONE

*N*ot surprisingly, studies draw causal links between prayer and faith and health and happiness. Dr. Harold G. Koenig of Duke University concluded, based on an exhaustive analysis of more than fifteen hundred reputable medical studies, that "people who are more religious and pray more have better mental and physical health." He went on to say that spiritual people, those who pursue divine assistance, "cope with stress better, they experience greater well-being because they have more hope, they're more optimistic, they experience less depression, less anxiety, and they commit suicide less often."[1]

Pray for one another, that you may be healed.

—James 5:16

Write down a prayer for someone else. Notice how this makes you feel.

....

....

....

....

....

....

....

....

....

....

....

....

When we seek
to bless others
through prayer,
we are blessed.

THIRTY-TWO

he act of praying for others has a boomerang effect. It allows us to shift the burden we carry for others to the shoulders of God. He invites us to cast all our cares upon him (1 Peter 5:7). Don't fret about politicians. Pray for them. Don't grow angry at the condition of the church. Pray for her. Don't let the difficulties of life suck you under. Give them to God before they get to you.

Rather than fretting about the future of your family, pray for them. Rather than assuming you can do nothing to help others, assume the posture of prayer.

Humble yourselves under the mighty hand of God, that He may exalt you in due time, casting all your care upon Him, for He cares for you.

—1 Peter 5:6–7

What are you worried about today? Lift that concern up to God by writing it down in prayer. Read the prayer aloud when you are finished. Return to this prayer anytime you start to worry about this circumstance.

. . . .

. . . .

. . . .

. . . .

. . . .

. . . .

. . . .

. . . .

. . . .

. . . .   *Impossible burdens*

. . . .   *are made bearable*

. . . .   *because we pray*

. . . .   *about them.*

THIRTY-THREE

*C*hrist himself prays (Hebrews 7:25). And he invites us to pray with him. "You also, as living stones, are being built up a spiritual house, a holy priesthood, to offer up spiritual sacrifices acceptable to God through Jesus Christ" (1 Peter 2:5). The job of the Old Testament priest was to intercede for his people before God. So in our intercession we function as priests, standing in the gap between the people of earth and God.

You actually have a "seat with [Christ] in the heavens" (Ephesians 2:6 NCV). You speak on behalf of your family, neighborhood, or softball team. Your sphere of influence is your region.

Because Jesus lives forever, he has a permanent priesthood. Therefore he is able to save completely those who come to God through him, because he always lives to intercede for them.

—Hebrews 7:24–25 NIV

How does it make you feel to know Jesus prays for you?

....

....

....

....

When God

....

burdens you

....

with a concern,

....

respond to these

....

promptings

....

by prayer.

....

....

....

....

....

....

*n*othing activates happiness like intercessory ministry. Try it. Next time you walk through a crowded airport, lift up your heart to heaven and pray something like this: *Lord, bless that man in the gray suit. He appears to be frazzled. And give strength to the mom and the infant. Look with mercy upon those military personnel.* Before you know it, a humdrum hike becomes a significant stroll of faith.

You will feel the same energy my brother and I felt as we helped Dad build the house! Your Father will hear you.

> The LORD is close to everyone who prays to him,
> to all who truly pray to him.
>
> —Psalm 145:18 NCV

Next time you are in a crowded place, begin praying for those around you, whether you know them or not. Record how this affected your mood.

....

....

....

....

....

....

....

....

....

....

....   *We can do much*

....   *after we pray, but*

....   *we can do nothing*

....   *until we pray.*

Find Happiness by Serving Others

The world is full of quiet servants. Perhaps you are one of them. Someone who works behind the scenes, sweeps the floors when the office doors are locked, carts the kids around from school to practice to games. You don't get paid much, if at all. You receive little recognition, and yet the Bible says those who serve will be considered great (Matthew 20:26).

This belief rubs against the grain of a culture that celebrates freedom—from obligations, your mortgage, your job—rather than service as a means to happiness. But scripture tells us that in Christ we are already free, "free from the law of sin and death" (Romans 8:2). Scripture also tells us how to use this freedom. As Paul wrote, "Do not use liberty as an opportunity for the flesh, but through love serve one another" (Galatians 5:13).

Freedom in Christ frees us to serve. Service might not sound like freedom, or happiness, to you, but when you have experienced the sacrificial love of Christ, serving others is not an obligation; it is a joyful response to the freedom you've been given. This is why the janitor in the building can be happier than the CEO and why a parent in a minivan might be happier than the hotshot in a Porsche. They have discovered the joy of serving in the name of Christ.

Feeling low on happiness? Ask others what they need. Serve them first, not because you have to but because you are free to.

THIRTY-FIVE

*Q*uiet servants. The supporting cast of the kingdom of God. They seek to do what is right. They show up. Open doors. Cook dinners. Visit the sick. You seldom see them in front of an audience. That's the last place most of them want to be. They don't stand behind a pulpit; they make sure the pulpit is there. They don't wear a microphone but make certain it's turned on.

They embody this verse: "For you, brethren, have been called to liberty; only do not use liberty as an opportunity for the flesh, but through love serve one another" (Galatians 5:13).

> You, brethren, have been called to liberty; only do not use liberty as an opportunity for the flesh, but through love serve one another.
>
> —Galatians 5:13

Do you know any quiet servants? Describe that person and what you like about him or her. If you are a quiet servant yourself, what motivates you to serve others?

....

....

....

....

....

....

....

....

....

....

....

....

In a society that seeks to be served, we seek opportunities to serve others.

THIRTY-SIX

*F*or the first five chapters of Galatians, the apostle Paul proclaimed, "You are free! Free from sin. Free from guilt. Free from rules. Free from regulations. The yoke of slavery is off, and the liberation has begun." Our freedom, however, is not an excuse for us to do whatever we want. Just the opposite. We voluntarily indenture ourselves to others. In a society that seeks to be served, we seek opportunities to serve others.

Be sure to fear the LORD and serve him faithfully with all your heart; consider what great things he has done for you.

—1 Samuel 12:24 NIV

Do you feel free to serve others, or does serving feel like an obligation? Explain your response.

....

....

....

....

....

....

....

....

....

....

....

....

Because we are free, we can serve.

THIRTY-SEVEN

It was the servant spirit of Mary that led God to select her to be the mother of Jesus. She wasn't a scholar or a sophisticated socialite. She was simple. Plain. A peasant. She hailed from Nazareth, a dusty village in an oppressed district in Galilee.

In the social strata of her day, Mary occupied the lowest step. As a Jew she answered to the Romans. As a female she was subservient to males. As a young girl she was second to older women. She was poor, so she was beneath the upper class.

Mary was extraordinarily ordinary. Yet this virtue set her apart: "I am the servant of the Lord" (Luke 1:38 NCV).

Mary said, "I am the servant of the Lord. Let this happen to me as you say!"

—Luke 1:38 NCV

Why do you think God chooses servant-hearted people to carry out his will?

....

....

....

....

....

....

....

....

....

....

God can

....

use you.

....

THIRTY-EIGHT

*A*ndrew was a servant who lived in the shadow of others. He was the brother of Peter. He came from the same town as James and John. Yet when we discuss the inner circle of Peter, James, and John, we don't mention Andrew. His name never appears at the top of the list of leaders.

Quiet, however, does not mean complacent. Just because Andrew avoided the limelight doesn't mean he lacked fire. He led his brother Peter to Jesus. Peter led the Jerusalem church. He defended the apostle Paul. Anyone who appreciates Paul's epistles owes a debt of gratitude to Peter. And anyone who has benefited from the rocklike faith of Peter owes a debt to the servant spirit of Andrew.

"Whoever desires to become great among you, let him be your servant."

—Matthew 20:26

Do you ever desire greatness in your job, social status, or among your circle of friends? How could the definition of greatness in Matthew 20:26 change these goals and desires?

....

....

....

....

....   *When God wants*

....   *to bring Christ*

....   *into the world, he*

....   *looks for servants.*

....

....

....

....

....

....

THIRTY-NINE

*I*n one of Jesus' appearances to his followers, they were on the Sea of Galilee when they heard him call out from the shore. When he told them where to find fish, they realized it was Jesus. Peter plunged into the water and swam to shore. The other disciples grabbed their oars and paddled. When they reached the beach, they saw the most extraordinary sight. Jesus was cooking! He told them, "Come and eat breakfast" (John 21:12).

Shouldn't the roles be reversed? He, the unrivaled Commander of the Universe, wore the apron?

"Even the Son of Man came not to be served but to serve, and to give his life as a ransom for many."

—Mark 10:45 ESV

Do you think of Jesus as a servant? What feelings, thoughts, or images come to mind when you think about Jesus serving the disciples?

....

....

....

....

....

....

....

....

....

.... *Jesus*

.... *came to*

.... *serve.*

$\mathcal{S}$uppose you took a servant role. Be the family member who offers to wash the dishes after dinner. Be the colleague who serves the staff by arriving on time for each meeting and listening attentively. Be the neighbor who mows the grass of the elderly couple.

Can you imagine the joy-giving benefits of these decisions?

Of course you can! You've experienced it. When you took a pie to the sick coworker or sang a song to the sick child, were not both of you encouraged because of it? You've been unScrooged from stinginess enough times to know the easiest way to make yourself smile is to make someone else smile first.

Whatever you do, work heartily, as for the Lord and not for men, knowing that from the Lord you will receive the inheritance as your reward. You are serving the Lord Christ.

—Colossians 3:23–24 ESV

List a few simple acts of service you could do for the people in your life. Record how serving others—without expecting them to serve you in return—affects your happiness level.

....

....

....

....   *It is in your*

....   *best interest to*

....   *look out for the*

....   *interest of others.*

....

....

....

....

....

....

....

Find Happiness in Forgiveness

When someone hurts you, anger, revenge, and retaliation are natural human responses. This is why forgiveness is perhaps the most difficult of the "one another" passages in the Bible. Love one another? Okay. Greet one another? Sure. But with Paul's instruction to "forgive one another" (Ephesians 4:32 ESV), we hesitate. How can we forgive what our offender did or said? How can we simply let go of the hurt he or she caused? Forgiveness is perhaps the most difficult one-another passage, but it also might be the most important.

Nothing will hamper your happiness like harboring a grudge. When we remain angry toward the one who hurt us, rarely does it change that person, but it does change us. Resentment wears on the mind, body, and soul, trapping us in past pain and hurt. Forgiveness, on the other hand, paves a path forward.

Paul wrote in Romans, "All have sinned and fall short of the glory of God, and all are justified freely by his grace through the redemption that came by Christ Jesus" (Romans 3:23–24 NIV). We forgive not because we are no longer hurt or upset or because our offender deserves it. We forgive simply because we have been forgiven. Only when we believe this will we be able to let our offender off the hook. And only when we let him off the hook will we find happiness.

A grudge cripples you; forgiveness frees you. The former says happiness can't happen because of the hurt. The latter says happiness can happen in spite of the hurt. Which will you choose today?

FORTY-ONE

*S*ome people abandon the path of forgiveness because they perceive it to be impossibly steep. So let's be realistic about the act. Forgiveness does not pardon the offense, excuse the misdeed, or ignore it. Forgiveness is not necessarily reconciliation. A reestablished relationship with the transgressor is not essential or always even possible. Even more, the phrase "forgive and forget" sets an unreachable standard. Painful memories are not like old clothing. They defy easy shedding.

Forgiveness is simply the act of changing your attitude toward the offender; it's moving from a desire to harm toward an openness to be at peace.

Be kind to one another, tenderhearted, forgiving one another, even as God in Christ forgave you.

—Ephesians 4:32

Write about someone in your life you need to forgive. Why haven't you forgiven this person? What could forgiveness look like in this particular circumstance?

....

....

....

....

....

....

....

....

....

....

....

....   *left unchecked,*

....   *grudges send us on*

....   *a downward spiral.*

FORTY-TWO

When researchers from Duke University listed eight factors that promote emotional stability, four of them related to forgiveness.

1. Avoiding suspicion and resentment.
2. Not living in the past.
3. Not wasting time and energy fighting conditions that can't be changed.
4. Refusing to indulge in self-pity when handed a raw deal.[1]

In a paper titled "Granting Forgiveness or Harboring Grudges," researchers relate how they invited people to reflect on a person who had caused them harm. Just the thought of the perpetrator led to sweaty palms, facial muscle tension, a higher heart rate, and increased blood pressure. When subjects were instructed to imagine the possibility of forgiveness, all the above physiological issues were reversed.[2]

It is foolish to harbor a grudge.

—Ecclesiastes 7:9 GNT

Write about a time you let go of a grudge against someone else. How did you feel after you let go? What helped you forgive that person?

....

....

....   *A step in the direction*

....   *of forgiveness is a*

....   *decisive step toward*

....   *happiness.*

....

....

....

....

....

....

....

$\mathcal{H}$ e poured water into a basin and began to wash the disciples' feet, and to wipe them with the towel with which He was girded" (John 13:5).

This was the eve of the crucifixion and Jesus' final meal with his followers. Later that night the disciples realized the enormity of this gesture. They had pledged to stay with their Master, but those pledges melted like wax in the heat of the Roman torches.

I envision them sprinting until, depleted of strength, they plopped to the ground and let their heads fall forward as they looked wearily at the dirt. That's when they saw the feet Jesus had just washed. Jesus forgave his betrayers before they betrayed him.

Jesus, knowing that the Father had given all things into His hands, and that He had come from God and was going to God, rose from supper and laid aside His garments, took a towel and girded Himself. After that, He poured water into a basin and began to wash the disciples' feet, and to wipe them with the towel with which He was girded.

—John 13:3–5

Imagine you were one of the disciples in the Upper Room that night. How would you feel if Jesus washed your feet? What would your reaction be? What would you say to him, if anything?

....

....

....

....   *Because Jesus*

....   *knew who he*

....   *was, he could do*

....   *what he did.*

....

....

....

....

....

FORTY-FOUR

*S*uppose I were somehow to come into possession of your sin-history video. Every contrary act. Every wayward thought. Every reckless word. Would you want me to play it on a screen? By no means. You'd beg me not to. And I would beg you not to show mine.

Don't worry. I don't have it. But Jesus does. He's seen it. He's seen every backstreet, backseat, backhanded moment of our lives. And he has resolved, "My grace is enough. I can cleanse these people. I will wash away their betrayals."

He can be depended on to forgive us and to cleanse us from every wrong.

—1 John 1:9 TLB

Have you experienced the forgiveness of God through Jesus
Christ? If so, write about when you first felt forgiven by
him and how that changed you. If not, write about why
you might be hesitant to accept God's forgiveness. Be as
honest as you can be.

Before we knew we needed grace, we were offered it.

FORTY-FIVE

*L*et others bicker and fight; we don't.

Let others seek revenge; we don't.

Let others keep a list of offenders; we don't.

We take the towel. We fill the basin. We wash one another's feet.

Jesus could do this because he knew who he was—sent from and destined for heaven. And you? Do you know who you are? You are the creation of a good God, made in his image. You are destined to reign in an eternal kingdom. You are only heartbeats away from heaven.

Throw aside the robe of rights and expectation and make the most courageous of moves.

"If I then, your Lord and Teacher, have washed your feet, you also ought to wash one another's feet. For I have given you an example, that you should do as I have done to you."

—John 13:14–15

Imagine you are washing the feet of your offender, perhaps the one you wrote about during week 41. What do you need to tell this person? How could feeling secure in the forgiveness of Christ help you wash this person's feet?

....

....

....

Secure in who you

....

are, you can do

....

what Jesus did.

....

....

....

....

....

....

....

FORTY-SIX

*Y*ou've not been sprinkled with forgiveness. You've not been spattered with grace. You've not been dusted with kindness. You've been immersed in forgiveness, submerged in grace. Can you, standing as you are, shoulder-high in God's ocean of grace, not fill a cup and offer the happiness of forgiveness to others?

Happiness happens when you offer to others the grace you've been given. It's time to follow the example of Jesus in the Upper Room. It's time to forgive, just as God, in Christ, forgave you.

"Though your sins are like scarlet,
They shall be as white as snow;
Though they are red like crimson,
They shall be as wool."

—Isaiah 1:18

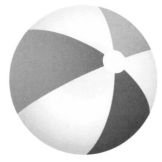

Spend some time reflecting on God's forgiveness toward you. Let his love wash over you. Let his forgiveness fully cover you. Write down a prayer in response.

....

....

....

....

....

....

....

....

....

....

....

....   *Happiness happens when you offer to others the grace you've been given.*

....

Find Happiness in the Love of God

A world without love is a world without happiness. What would we write songs about, watch movies about, read about? What would inspire us? The greatest muse for songwriters and poets truly is what "makes the world go 'round."

But as humans with flaws, we are not always good at loving others, even the ones we're married to. We get tired and cranky. We feel angry and disappointed. We feel depleted of love. This is when we must return to the source of love.

John wrote, "We love [God] because He first loved us" (1 John 4:19). Who loved first? God. The love of God changes us. It fills us. It gives us a new identity and sense of worth. Because of this, when we believe we are loved by God, we can love others.

Love is easy when it begins with God, but if we try to love without first being loved, we are like a car running on an empty tank, a river flowing during a drought. We have nothing to give. We can try and force it. We can try and muster love for others, but we won't last long. In order to truly love, we must let God love us first.

Over the next few weeks, think about how you could love the people around you, but also think about how you have been loved by God. Dwell in the safety of God's love, allow yourself to be filled with it, and watch as his great love for you overflows onto those around you.

FORTY-SEVEN

*D*iscover the purest source of happiness, the love of God. A love that is "too wonderful to be measured" (Ephesians 3:19 CEV). A love that is not regulated by the receiver. What Moses said to Israel is what God says to us: "The Lord did not set his heart on you and choose you because you were more numerous than other nations, for you were the smallest of all nations! Rather, it was simply that the Lord loves you" (Deuteronomy 7:7–8 NLT).

Does he love us because of our goodness? Because of our kindness? Because of our great devotion? No, he loves us because of *his* goodness, kindness, and great devotion.

I want you to know all about Christ's love, although it is too wonderful to be measured. Then your lives will be filled with all that God is.

—Ephesians 3:19 CEV

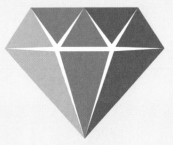

How would you describe the love of God? Write down any word, phrase, or image that comes to mind when you think about God's love.

....

....

....

....

....

....

....

....

....

....

It is only by receiving

....

our Father's love that

....

we can discover a

....

love for others.

FORTY-EIGHT

ave you let God love you? Please don't hurry past the question. Have you let God's love seep into the innermost recesses of your life? Have you, as John wrote, "come to know [by . . . experience], and have believed . . . the love which God has for us" (1 John 4:16 AMP)?

If your answer is "Uh, I don't know" or "Well, it's been a while" or "I don't think God loves a person like me," then we just stumbled upon something.

We have known and believed the love that God has for us. God is love, and he who abides in love abides in God, and God in him.

—1 John 4:16

Have you let God love you? If so, write about when you first experienced the love of God and how it impacted you. If not, what is holding you back from fully believing in God's love?

Let God
love you!

FORTY-NINE

The reason God loves you is that he has chosen to love you. You are loved when you don't feel lovely. Others may abandon you, divorce you, and ignore you. God will love you. These are his words: "I'll call nobodies and make them somebodies; I'll call the unloved and make them beloved" (Romans 9:25 MSG).

Let this love happen in your life. Let this love give birth to the greatest joy: "I am beloved by heaven."

"And I will have mercy on her who had not obtained
    mercy;
Then I will say to those who were not My people,
'You are My people!'
And they shall say, 'You are my God!'"

—Hosea 2:23

What do you think about the idea that God loves you simply because he chose to love you? Does it make you uncomfortable, happy, confused? Write down your thoughts.

....

....

....

....

....

....

....

....

....

....   *You are loved by*

....   *God even when*

....   *you are loved by*

....   *no one else.*

FIFTY

I find at least eleven appearances of the "love one another" admonition. Three by Christ (John 13:34; 15:12, 17). Three by Paul (Romans 13:8; 1 Thessalonians 3:12; 4:9). One by Peter (1 Peter 1:22) and four by the apostle John (1 John 3:11; 4:7, 11; 2 John v. 5).

The Greek word used for *love* (*agape*) in these passages denotes an unselfish affection.[1] *Agape* love writes the check when the balance is low, forgives the mistake when the offense is high, offers patience when stress is abundant, and extends kindness when kindness is rare. "For God so loved [*agapaó*] the world that he gave his one and only Son" (John 3:16 NIV).

"This is My commandment, that you love one another as I have loved you. Greater love has no one than this, than to lay down one's life for his friends."

—John 15:12–13

How is *agape* love different from the romantic love shown in the media and pop culture?

. . . .

. . . .

. . . .

. . . .

. . . .

. . . .

. . . .

. . . .

. . . .

. . . .   *Agape*

. . . .   *love*

. . . .   *gives.*

FIFTY-ONE

*W*e don't love people because people are lovable. People can be cranky, stubborn, selfish, and cruel. We love people for this reason: we have come to experience and believe the love that God has for us.

We tend to skip this step. "I'm supposed to love my neighbor? All right, by golly, I will." We clench our teeth and redouble our efforts as if there were within us a distillery of affection. If we poke it and prod it and turn up the heat, another bottle of love will pour forth.

It won't! The source is not within us. It is only by receiving our Father's *agape* love that we can discover an *agape* love for others.

Beloved, if God so loved us, we also ought to love one another.

—1 John 4:11

Write about someone in your life who is difficult to love. What has been your strategy for loving this person? Have you tried to force it? Are you depending on God's love? Have you given up?

....

....

....

....

....

....

....

....

....

....   *Be loved.*

....   *Then love.*

FIFTY-TWO

*S*ettle yourself into the hammock of God's affection. And as you do, to the degree you do, you will give that love to others.

Perhaps names of people who are anything but lovable are surfacing in your mind. Maybe you've spent a decade cultivating a stubborn bias against him or nursing a grudge against her or indulging a pet prejudice against them.

Prepare yourself for a new day. As God has his way with you, as he loves through you, those old animosities and barbed-wire fences are going to come down. That's how happiness happens. God will not let you live with your old hatred and prejudices.

"If all you do is love the lovable, do you expect a bonus? Anybody can do that. If you simply say hello to those who greet you, do you expect a medal? Any run-of-the-mill sinner does that. In a word, what I'm saying is, *Grow up.* You're kingdom subjects. Now live like it. Live out your God-created identity. Live generously and graciously toward others, the way God lives toward you."

—Matthew 5:47–48 MSG

Write down a list of ways that God has shown his love for you. Spend some time reflecting on this list. How could "settling yourself in the hammock of God's affection" help you love others?

....

....

....

....   *Imagine the joy*

....   *you will find as*

....   *you learn to find*

                                                              joy in people.

....

....

....

....

....

....

SUN

Final Thoughts

*S*pend some time reflecting on the last year of journaling and learning about happiness.

What was this experience like for you?

....

....

....

....

....

....

....

....

....

....

What did you learn about happiness?

....

....

....

....

....

....

....

....

....

....

....

....

What did you learn about yourself?

....

....

....

....

....

....

....

....

....

....

....

....

What did you learn about others?

What did you learn about God?

....

....

....

....

....

....

....

....

....

....

....

....

Notes

Introduction

1. Alexandra Sifferlin, "Here's How Happy Americans Are Right Now," *Time*, July 26, 2017, http://time.com/4871720/how-happy-are-americans/.

Chapter 1

1. Randy Alcorn, *Happiness* (Carol Stream, IL: Tyndale, 2015), 19.

Part 2: Find Happiness by Encouraging One Another

1. W. E. Vine, *Vine's Expository Dictionary of New Testament Words: A Comprehensive Dictionary of the Original Greek Words with Their Precise Meanings for English Readers* (McLean, VA: MacDonald Publishing, n.d.), "Comfort, Comforter, Comfortless," 209–10.

Chapter 7

1. Ibid.

Chapter 12

1. Vine, *Vine's Expository Dictionary*, "Consider," 231–32.

Chapter 14

1. Vine, *Vine's Expository Dictionary*, "Longsuffering," 694.
2. David Hocking, "The Patience of God," Blue Letter Bible, https://www.blueletterbible.org/comm/hocking_david/attributes/attributes14.cfm.

Chapter 25

1. Sonja Lyubomirsky, *The How of Happiness: A Practical Approach to Getting the Life You Want* (London: Piatkus, 2007), 150–51.

Chapter 31

1. "Science Proves the Healing Power of Prayer," NewsmaxHealth, March 31, 2015, https://www.newsmax.com/health/headline/prayer-health-faith-medicine/2015/03/31/id/635623/.

Chapter 42

1. "Peace of Mind," a sociological study conducted by Duke University, cited in Rudy A. Magnan, *Reinventing American Education: Applying Innovative and Quality Thinking to Solving Problems in Education* (Bloomington, IN: Xlibris, 2010), 23. These are the other four: 1. Staying involved with the living world. 2. Cultivating old-fashioned virtues: love, humor, compassion, and loyalty. 3. Not expecting too much of oneself. 4. Finding something bigger than oneself to believe in.
2. Charlotte vanOyen Witvliet, Thomas E. Ludwig, and Kelly L. Vander Laan, "Granting Forgiveness or Harboring Grudges: Implications for Emotion, Physiology, and Health," *Psychological Science* 12, no. 2 (March 2001): 117–23, https://greatergood.berkeley.edu/images/uploads/VanOyenWitvliet-GrantingForgiveness.pdf.

Chapter 50

1. Vine, *Vine's Expository Dictionary*, "Love," 702.

About the Author

Since entering the ministry in 1978, Max Lucado has served churches in Miami, Florida; Rio de Janeiro, Brazil; and San Antonio, Texas. He currently serves as Teaching Minister of Oak Hills Church in San Antonio. He is America's bestselling inspirational author with more than 130 million books in print.

Follow Max on his website at MaxLucado.com and on Facebook, Instagram, and Twitter @MaxLucado.

Also by Max Lucado

Inspirational

3:16

A Gentle Thunder

A Love Worth Giving

And the Angels Were Silent

Anxious for Nothing

Because of Bethlehem

Before Amen

Come Thirsty

Cure for the Common Life

Facing Your Giants

Fearless

Glory Days

God Came Near

Grace

Great Day Every Day

He Chose the Nails

He Still Moves Stones

How Happiness Happens

In the Eye of the Storm

In the Grip of Grace

It's Not About Me

Just Like Jesus

Max on Life

More to Your Story

Next Door Savior

No Wonder They Call Him the Savior

On the Anvil

Outlive Your Life

Six Hours One Friday

The Applause of Heaven

The Great House of God

Traveling Light

Unshakable Hope

When Christ Comes

When God Whispers Your Name

You'll Get Through This

Fiction

Christmas Stories

Miracle at the Higher Grounds Café

The Christmas Candle

Bibles (General Editor)

Children's Daily Devotional Bible

Grace for the Moment Daily Bible

The Lucado Life Lessons Study Bible

Children's Books

A Max Lucado Children's Treasury

Do You Know I Love You, God?

God Always Keeps His Promises

God Forgives Me, and I Forgive You

God Listens When I Pray

Grace for the Moment: 365 Devotions for Kids

Hermie, a Common Caterpillar

I'm Not a Scaredy Cat

Itsy Bitsy Christmas

Just in Case You Ever Wonder

Lucado Treasury of Bedtime Prayers

One Hand, Two Hands

Thank You, God, for Blessing Me

Thank You, God, for Loving Me

The Boy and the Ocean

The Crippled Lamb

The Oak Inside the Acorn

The Tallest of Smalls

You Are Mine

You Are Special

Young Adult Books

3:16

It's Not About Me

Make Every Day Count

Unshakable Hope Promise Book

Wild Grace

You Were Made to Make a Difference

Gift Books

Fear Not Promise Book

For the Tough Times

God Thinks You're Wonderful

Grace for the Moment

Grace Happens Here

His Name Is Jesus

Let the Journey Begin

Live Loved

Mocha with Max

Praying the Promises

Safe in the Shepherd's Arms

This Is Love

You Changed My Life